BANARAS

THE ETERNAL FLAME OF ANCIENT SPIRITUALITY AND DIVINE CONNECTIONS UNCOVERED

ADITYA GUPTA

Dedication

Dedicated to my father, the late Shri. Arvind Kumar Gupta, who has now passed on to the abode of God and heaven. It was he who instilled in me the values of culture and ethics, and taught me to lead a disciplined life by understanding the joys and sorrows of others and living with humanity. His wisdom and guidance have been invaluable in shaping my character and inspiring me to strive towards excellence in all my endeavors.

May his soul rest in eternal peace.

ᐅᐅᐅ

Contents

Contents

Prayer

Ganggaa-Tarangga-Ramanniiya-Jattaa-Kalaapam
Gaurii-Nirantara-Vibhuushita-Vaama-Bhaagam
Naaraayanna-Priyam-Anangga-Madaa-
[A]pahaaram
Vaaraannasii-Pura-Patim Bhaja Vishvanaatham ||

❦❦❦

About The Author

Mr. Aditya Gupta is a young entrepreneur hailing from the city of Varanasi, Uttar Pradesh. He completed his MBA from the prestigious Banaras Hindu University and is currently managing his ancestral business. Mr. Gupta's passion for his hometown and its rich cultural heritage is evident in his involvement with numerous social and cultural activities in the city.

From a young age, Mr. Gupta was introduced to the cultural significance of Varanasi by his father, Arvind Kumar Gupta, who was a devoted lover of the city. It was this upbringing that instilled in him a deep love and appreciation for the city's heritage and traditions, and sparked his desire to share this with others.

In addition to his business pursuits, Mr. Gupta is deeply committed to promoting the cultural and social vibrancy of Varanasi. He is a regular participant in a wide range of cultural activities in the city, including music and dance performances, religious festivals, and charitable events. His dedication to preserving and promoting the traditions of Varanasi has earned him widespread recognition and respect among the local community.

It has always been Mr. Gupta's dream to share his love and dedication to the city of Varanasi with others through the written word. This dream has now been fulfilled with his latest book, which showcases his deep knowledge and appreciation for the city's rich cultural heritage. Through this book, Mr. Gupta hopes to inspire others to discover and appreciate the timeless wisdom and enduring teachings of Varanasi.

In addition to his work as an author and entrepreneur, Mr. Gupta remains actively engaged in promoting the social and cultural vibrancy of Varanasi. He continues to participate in a wide range of cultural activities in the city, and is committed to preserving and promoting the city's unique heritage and traditions for future generations to enjoy.

❧❧❧

Preface

Banaras, the spiritual capital of India, is a city that has been captivating the world for centuries with its rich culture, ancient traditions, and divine aura. This city has a unique place in the hearts of millions of people who visit it every year to experience the spirituality that permeates every corner of the city.

Through this book, "Banaras: The Eternal Flame of Ancient Spirituality and Divine Connections Uncovered," we aim to take our readers on a journey of discovery and exploration into the mystical world of Banaras. From the history and mythology of the city to the Ghats, from the sacred temples to the revered shrines, from the music and mantras to the Ayurveda and yoga, we will explore the many facets of this enchanting city.

We will also delve into the spiritual legacy of Banaras, the legacy that has been passed down from generation to generation through the guru-shishya parampara. We will examine the role of Banaras in shaping the Hindu philosophy and literature, and its significance as a center of Buddhism.

In this book, we will explore Banaras beyond its spiritual dimensions, taking a closer look at its cultural heritage, artistic treasures, and culinary delights. We will also reflect on the personal journeys of transformation and self-discovery that Banaras has inspired in many of its visitors.

We hope that this book will inspire you to explore Banaras and its spiritual legacy, and that it will provide a deeper understanding of the ancient traditions that have survived for centuries.

Aditya Gupta, Varanasi
20th March 2023

Prologue

We are proud that India got entry in G20 and also its presidency to hosting G20 summit in India in 2023. We the citizens of India are eager to explore everything about India to the world and this is book is one of my humble submission to that.

Jai Hind!

ᐅᐅᐅ

Disclaimer

The opinions expressed in this book are the sole opinions of the author and do not reflect the views of any organization or individual. The book is written with the intention of highlighting the positive aspects of the city of Banaras (Varanasi) and is not intended to offend or harm any individual or group. The author fully respects the right to freedom of speech and expression guaranteed by Article 19(1)(a) of the Constitution of India.

ONE

INTRODUCTION TO BANARAS: THE SPIRITUAL CAPITAL OF INDIA

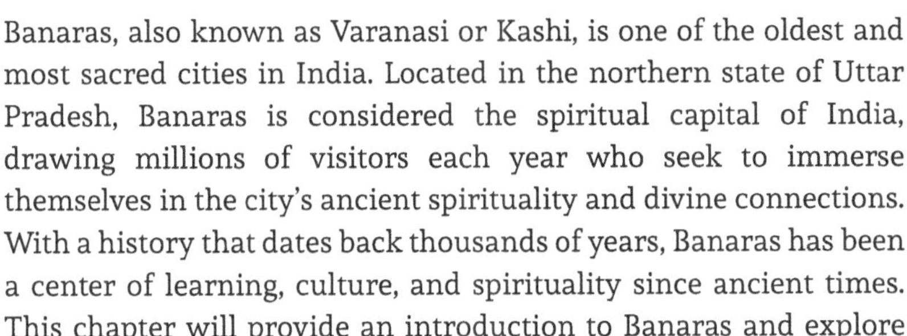

Banaras, also known as Varanasi or Kashi, is one of the oldest and most sacred cities in India. Located in the northern state of Uttar Pradesh, Banaras is considered the spiritual capital of India, drawing millions of visitors each year who seek to immerse themselves in the city's ancient spirituality and divine connections. With a history that dates back thousands of years, Banaras has been a center of learning, culture, and spirituality since ancient times. This chapter will provide an introduction to Banaras and explore some of the key aspects that make it such a special place.

History of Banaras

Banaras has a rich and ancient history that spans over three millennia. According to Hindu mythology, Lord Shiva founded the city around 5,000 years ago. The city is said to be situated at the spot where Lord Shiva and his wife Parvati stood when they created the world. Banaras has been mentioned in many ancient texts such as the Vedas, the Puranas, and the Ramayana. It has been a center of learning, culture, and spirituality for centuries, attracting scholars, poets, and spiritual seekers from all over India and beyond.

Culture of Banaras

Banaras has a unique culture that is steeped in tradition and spirituality. The city is famous for its rich classical music and dance traditions, which have been passed down through generations of musicians and performers. The Banaras gharana of classical music is renowned for its distinctive style and is considered one of the most important schools of Indian classical music. The city is also known for its handloom weaving, especially the famous Banarasi silk sarees, which are woven with intricate designs and patterns.

Spirituality of Banaras

Banaras is considered one of the most spiritual places in the world, with a deep and profound connection to the divine. The city is home to many temples and sacred sites, including the famous Kashi Vishwanath Temple, dedicated to Lord Shiva. The temple attracts millions of devotees each year who come to offer their prayers and seek blessings from the deity. Banaras is also home to many ashrams and spiritual centers, where seekers can engage in yoga, meditation, and other spiritual practices.

The Ghats of Banaras

One of the most iconic features of Banaras is its ghats, or riverfront steps, along the banks of the holy River Ganges. The ghats are a central part of life in Banaras, with locals and visitors alike flocking to them to take a dip in the sacred waters and perform rituals and ceremonies. The ghats are also the site of many important festivals and events, including the famous Ganga Aarti, a daily ceremony in which priests perform rituals and offer prayers to the river goddess.

To summarise, Banaras is a city that is steeped in spirituality and ancient tradition. Its rich history, culture, and spirituality make it a truly unique and special place. From the ghats of the River Ganges to the temples and ashrams that dot the city, Banaras is a place where seekers and pilgrims from all over the world come to connect with the divine and experience the eternal flame of ancient spirituality. As the spiritual capital of India, Banaras continues to inspire and captivate people from all walks of life, with its timeless wisdom and enduring teachings.

At the same time, Banaras is a city that is constantly evolving and adapting to modern times. It is a city that embraces change while also preserving its rich heritage and culture. From its bustling markets and vibrant music scene to its growing technology industry and world-class universities, Banaras is a city that is as dynamic as it is spiritual.

Yet despite all the changes that have taken place in Banaras over the years, one thing remains constant: the deep sense of spirituality and reverence that permeates every aspect of life in this ancient city. Whether you are a believer or a skeptic, a tourist or a resident, Banaras has a way of touching your soul and reminding you of the timeless wisdom and enduring truths that lie at the heart of all spiritual traditions.

So if you are looking for a place to connect with the divine, to explore the mysteries of the universe, and to experience the timeless teachings of the sages and saints, look no further than Banaras. This is a city that will inspire and uplift you, that will challenge and transform you, and that will leave an indelible imprint on your heart and soul."

ᐁᐁᐁ

*"Banaras is older than history, older than tradition,
older even than legend and looks twice as old as all
of them put together."*

Mark Twain

TWO

HISTORY AND MYTHOLOGY OF BANARAS

Banaras, also known as Varanasi, is one of the oldest living cities in the world. Located on the banks of the holy river Ganges, this city has a rich history and mythology that dates back thousands of years. Banaras is not only an important religious center for Hindus, but it is also a significant cultural hub that has attracted scholars, poets, writers, and artists for centuries.

The city of Banaras has been mentioned in various ancient texts and scriptures such as the Vedas, Puranas, Ramayana, and Mahabharata. According to Hindu mythology, Lord Shiva, the destroyer of the universe, founded Banaras. Legend has it that when Lord Shiva and his wife Parvati were returning from a trip, they decided to rest in the city, which was then a dense forest. Impressed by the beauty of the place, Lord Shiva decided to make it his abode. Thus, Banaras became known as the city of Lord Shiva.

Over time, Banaras became an important center of learning and spirituality. Many renowned scholars and sages, such as Patanjali,

Adi Shankaracharya, Kabir, Tulsidas, and Ramanuja, have lived and taught in this city. It is also believed that the famous Chinese traveler and writer, Hiuen Tsang, visited Banaras in the 7th century AD and wrote extensively about the city's culture and traditions.

Banaras has played an essential role in the development of Hinduism as a religion. Many Hindu temples and shrines are located in the city, and thousands of pilgrims visit these sites every year. One of the most famous temples in Banaras is the Kashi Vishwanath Temple, dedicated to Lord Shiva. This temple has been destroyed and rebuilt many times over the centuries, and the current structure was built in 1780 by the Maratha ruler, Maharani Ahilya Bai Holkar.

Apart from the Kashi Vishwanath Temple, there are many other important temples in Banaras, such as the Sankat Mochan Hanuman Temple, the Durga Temple, the Tulsi Manas Temple, and the Bharat Mata Temple. The city is also famous for its ghats, which are a series of steps leading down to the river Ganges. The ghats are a popular site for rituals, ceremonies, and religious bathing. The most famous ghat in Banaras is the Dashashwamedh Ghat, which is believed to be the spot where Lord Brahma performed a grand sacrifice.

Banaras has also been an important center for art and culture. The city is known for its silk saris, which are handwoven using intricate designs and patterns. Many traditional music and dance forms, such as Bharatnatyam, Kathak, and Hindustani classical music, originated in Banaras. The city has also produced many famous writers, poets, and artists, such as Kabir, Tulsidas, Ravi Shankar, and Girija Devi.

In conclusion, Banaras is a city that is steeped in history, mythology, and spirituality. It has played a significant role in the development of Hinduism as a religion and has been a hub of learning, culture, and art for centuries. Banaras is a city that has inspired countless artists, scholars, and seekers, and it continues to attract visitors from all over the world who come to experience the city's unique energy and spirit.

ᐅᐅᐅ

"Banaras is the center of Hindu civilization, the fountain of all spiritual knowledge."

Mahatma Gandhi

⊳⊳⊳

THREE

KASHI VISHWANATH TEMPLE: THE MOST REVERED SHRINE IN BANARAS

The Kashi Vishwanath Temple is the most revered and significant shrine in Banaras. This ancient temple is dedicated to Lord Shiva, who is known as the destroyer of the universe in Hindu mythology. The temple is located in the heart of the city, near the banks of the river Ganges, and is visited by millions of devotees every year.

The history of the Kashi Vishwanath Temple dates back to the 11th century when it was originally built by King Harishchandra. Over the centuries, the temple was destroyed and rebuilt many times by various rulers, including the Mughals and the Marathas. The current structure of the temple was built in 1780 by the Maratha ruler, Maharani Ahilyabai Holkar, who was a great devotee of Lord Shiva.

The Kashi Vishwanath Temple is one of the twelve Jyotirlingas, which are considered to be the most sacred abodes of Lord Shiva.

According to Hindu mythology, the Jyotirlingas were created by Lord Shiva himself, and they are believed to be the source of divine energy and spiritual power. The Kashi Vishwanath Temple is considered to be one of the most powerful Jyotirlingas, and it is believed that a visit to this temple can purify the soul and bring blessings and good fortune.

The main deity of the Kashi Vishwanath Temple is a lingam, which is a symbolic representation of Lord Shiva. The lingam is situated in the sanctum sanctorum of the temple and is bathed with holy water and milk several times a day. The lingam is believed to be one of the twelve Jyotirlingas, and it is said to be the center of the universe and the source of all divine energy.

The Kashi Vishwanath Temple is also known for its elaborate architecture and intricate carvings. The temple has a large courtyard surrounded by several smaller shrines dedicated to various deities. The walls of the temple are adorned with intricate carvings of Hindu gods and goddesses, and the ceiling is decorated with beautiful paintings and murals.

The temple complex also houses several smaller temples and shrines, such as the Annapurna Temple, the Vishalakshi Temple, and the Kalabhairav Temple. These temples are dedicated to various deities and are considered to be important centers of worship in their own right.

The Kashi Vishwanath Temple is also famous for its unique rituals and traditions. One of the most popular rituals is the daily Ganga Aarti, which is a grand ceremony held on the banks of the river Ganges every evening. The Aarti involves the chanting of hymns, the lighting of lamps, and the offering of flowers and incense to the river Ganges. The Aarti is considered to be a powerful spiritual experience, and it attracts thousands of devotees and tourists every day.

In conclusion, the Kashi Vishwanath Temple is the most revered and significant shrine in Banaras. It is a center of faith and spirituality, and a place where devotees come to seek blessings and spiritual guidance. The temple is not only an important religious site but also a symbol of Banaras's rich history and culture. A visit to the Kashi Vishwanath Temple is a must for anyone seeking to experience the unique energy and spiritual power of Banaras.

*"Banaras is the oldest living city in the world, a city
that has been in existence for over 5,000 years."*

J. Krishnamurti

ᐁᐁᐁ

FOUR

GHATS OF BANARAS: A JOURNEY THROUGH SACRED WATERS

The Ghats of Banaras are perhaps the most iconic and recognizable feature of the city. These are the series of steps that lead down to the banks of the River Ganges, where people come to bathe, perform rituals, and seek spiritual solace. The Ghats are an integral part of Banaras's culture and history and have been witness to countless important events and moments in the city's past.

The Ghats of Banaras are believed to number over 80, and each has its own unique history and significance. The most famous of these Ghats are the Dashashwamedh Ghat, the Manikarnika Ghat, and the Harishchandra Ghat. The Dashashwamedh Ghat is the most popular Ghat and is considered to be the main Ghat in Banaras. It is also the site of the daily Ganga Aarti, which is a grand ceremony held every evening to honor the river Ganges.

The Ghats of Banaras are steeped in mythology and legend.

According to Hindu mythology, Lord Shiva and his wife, Parvati, once stood on the banks of the river Ganges and watched the world go by. It is said that the city of Banaras was born from this moment, and the Ghats were built to honor this divine event. The Ghats are also believed to be the site of many other important events in Hindu mythology, such as the birth of Lord Rama and the great battle of Mahabharata.

The Ghats of Banaras have always been an important center of pilgrimage for Hindus. It is believed that a dip in the holy waters of the river Ganges can wash away one's sins and purify the soul. Millions of devotees come to the Ghats every year to take a dip in the river and perform various rituals and offerings. The Ghats are also an important site for the performance of last rites and cremation ceremonies, and the Manikarnika Ghat is considered to be the most sacred site for this purpose.

The Ghats of Banaras are also a testament to the city's rich cultural heritage. The Ghats are lined with beautiful temples, palaces, and mansions, many of which date back centuries. These buildings are important examples of Banaras's unique architecture and art and are considered to be important cultural heritage sites. The Ghats are also home to various markets and bazaars, where one can buy everything from silk saris to religious offerings.

The Ghats of Banaras are not just a physical space but also a cultural and social hub. The Ghats are a place where people come to meet, converse, and share stories. They are a space where people of different religions, castes, and social classes come together in harmony. The Ghats are also a place where artists, musicians, and poets come to perform and share their talents.

In conclusion, the Ghats of Banaras are an integral part of the city's culture, history, and spirituality. They are a symbol of the city's unique blend of mythology, religion, and culture. The Ghats are not just a physical space but also a social, cultural, and spiritual hub. A journey through the Ghats of Banaras is a journey through the sacred waters of the river Ganges and a glimpse into the soul of this ancient and spiritual city.

ᎠᎠᎠ

"Banaras is a city that is both ancient and eternal,
a city where the past and the present coexist in
perfect harmony."

Narendra Modi

❧❧❧

FIVE

THE ETERNAL FLAME OF GANGA AARTI

The Ganga Aarti is one of the most iconic and mesmerizing rituals performed in the city of Banaras. This ceremony is held every evening on the banks of the River Ganges and is a grand celebration of the holy river and its significance in Hindu mythology and spirituality. The Ganga Aarti is a visual and spiritual spectacle that draws millions of tourists and devotees to Banaras every year.

The Ganga Aarti is performed at the Dashashwamedh Ghat, which is considered to be the main Ghat in Banaras. The ceremony is led by a group of priests who perform a series of rituals and offerings in front of a large gathering of devotees. The priests hold flaming lamps and dance to the rhythm of devotional songs and mantras, creating a surreal and spiritual atmosphere.

The Ganga Aarti is a celebration of the River Ganges and its significance in Hindu mythology and spirituality. The river Ganges is considered to be the holiest river in India and is believed to have the power to purify one's soul and wash away their sins. It is believed that a dip in the holy waters of the river Ganges can grant salvation and liberation from the cycle of birth and death. The Ganga Aarti is a way to honor and thank the river Ganges for its blessings and divine grace.

The Ganga Aarti is not just a religious ceremony but also a cultural and social event. The ceremony attracts people of all ages and backgrounds who come together to witness and participate in this grand celebration. The Ganga Aarti is a symbol of Banaras's unique culture and spirit of unity and harmony. The ceremony is performed in front of a large gathering of people who are united in their devotion and love for the river Ganges.

The Ganga Aarti is also a visual spectacle that is truly mesmerizing. The ceremony is performed against the backdrop of the river Ganges, which is illuminated by the flames of the lamps held by the priests. The dance of the priests and the rhythm of the devotional songs create a surreal and spiritual atmosphere that is both calming and uplifting. The Ganga Aarti is a feast for the senses and an experience that stays with you forever.

The Ganga Aarti is not just a ritual but also a way of life for the people of Banaras. The ceremony is performed every day, without fail, regardless of the weather or the number of people in attendance. The Ganga Aarti is a symbol of the city's eternal flame of spirituality and its deep-rooted connection with the river Ganges. The ceremony is a reminder of the city's ancient and spiritual heritage and its commitment to preserving and passing on its cultural traditions to future generations.

In conclusion, the Ganga Aarti is a grand and mesmerizing ceremony that captures the spirit and soul of the city of Banaras. It is a celebration of the holy river Ganges and its significance in Hindu mythology and spirituality. The Ganga Aarti is a visual and spiritual spectacle that draws millions of tourists and devotees to Banaras every year. It is a symbol of the city's unique culture and spirit of unity and harmony and a testament to its ancient and spiritual heritage. The Ganga Aarti is a celebration of life and a reminder of the eternal flame of spirituality that burns bright in the heart of Banaras.

ӬӬӬ

"Banaras is a city that is steeped in spirituality and culture, a city that has been inspiring artists, poets, and philosophers for centuries."

Amitabh Bachchan

SIX

The Enchanting Sound of Banaras: Music and Mantras

The city of Banaras is not just a place, but an experience that engages all the senses. It is a city that has a rich cultural and spiritual heritage that is manifested in its music and mantras. Music is an integral part of the city's life, and it is believed that the divine sound of music and mantras can uplift the soul and connect one to the divine. In this chapter, we explore the enchanting sound of Banaras, its music, and its mantras.

Banaras has a rich and diverse musical tradition that is rooted in its spiritual and cultural heritage. The city has produced some of the most renowned musicians and singers in India. The music of Banaras is a unique blend of classical, folk, and devotional music that is deeply connected to the city's spiritual and cultural identity. The music of Banaras is not just an art form, but a way of life that is deeply ingrained in the city's daily routine.

The most iconic musical instrument of Banaras is the sitar, which is widely regarded as one of the most beautiful and soulful musical instruments in the world. The sitar is often accompanied by the tabla, a percussion instrument that is an integral part of Indian classical music. The sound of the sitar and tabla is a perfect blend of melody and rhythm that is truly mesmerizing. The music of Banaras is not limited to classical music, but also includes folk music and devotional music that is often heard in the temples and shrines of the city.

In Banaras, music is not just a form of entertainment but also a way of connecting with the divine. The city is home to some of the most renowned music schools and academies that teach classical music and devotional music to students from all over the world. The city also hosts various music festivals and concerts that showcase the city's rich musical heritage.

One of the most captivating sounds in Banaras is the sound of the mantras. Mantras are sacred chants that are believed to have the power to connect one to the divine. The city is home to numerous temples and shrines where mantras are chanted continuously throughout the day. The most popular mantras in Banaras are the Mahamrityunjaya mantra, the Gayatri mantra, and the Om Namah Shivaya mantra. The sound of the mantras is a soothing and uplifting experience that can calm the mind and uplift the soul.

In Banaras, music and mantras are not just a form of entertainment or religious ritual but a way of life that is deeply ingrained in the city's culture and spirituality. The enchanting sound of Banaras is a celebration of life and a reminder of the eternal flame of spirituality that burns bright in the heart of the city.

In conclusion, the enchanting sound of Banaras is a reflection of the city's rich cultural and spiritual heritage. The music of Banaras is a unique blend of classical, folk, and devotional music that is deeply connected to the city's identity. The sound of the mantras is a reminder of the city's devotion and connection to the divine. The enchanting sound of Banaras is not just a sound but an experience that engages all the senses and uplifts the soul. It is a celebration of life and a testament to the city's eternal flame of spirituality.

"Banaras is the city where time stands still, and where the soul is free to roam."

William Dalrymple

❧❧❧

SEVEN

THE GURU-SHISHYA PARAMPARA: THE LEGACY OF SPIRITUAL TEACHERS IN BANARAS

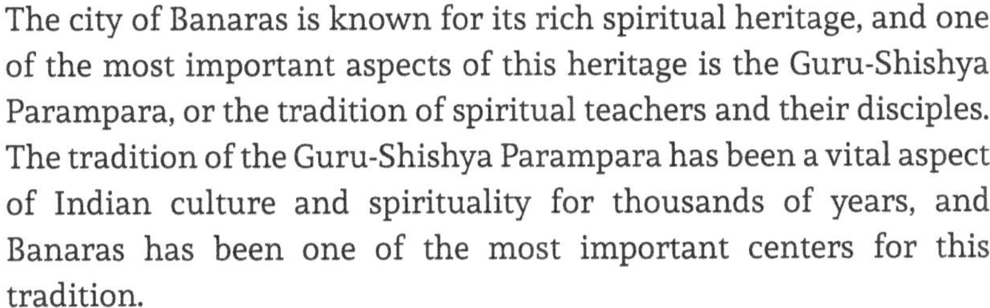

The city of Banaras is known for its rich spiritual heritage, and one of the most important aspects of this heritage is the Guru-Shishya Parampara, or the tradition of spiritual teachers and their disciples. The tradition of the Guru-Shishya Parampara has been a vital aspect of Indian culture and spirituality for thousands of years, and Banaras has been one of the most important centers for this tradition.

The Guru-Shishya Parampara is a relationship between a spiritual teacher and their disciple, where the teacher passes on their knowledge, wisdom, and experience to the disciple. The relationship is based on mutual respect, trust, and devotion. The spiritual teacher is known as the Guru, and the disciple is known as the Shishya. This tradition has been passed down from generation to generation, and it has been instrumental in preserving and transmitting the spiritual knowledge and practices of India.

Banaras has been home to many great spiritual teachers, who have left a lasting legacy on the city and the world. One of the most revered spiritual teachers in Banaras was Adi Shankaracharya, who was a great philosopher and theologian of ancient India. He established a monastery in Banaras, which became a center for spiritual learning and practice. He is also credited with establishing the Advaita Vedanta school of philosophy, which is one of the most influential schools of thought in India.

Another great spiritual teacher in Banaras was Swami Sivananda, who was a disciple of Swami Vishwananda Saraswati. He founded the Divine Life Society, which is an organization dedicated to the spiritual upliftment of humanity. He wrote many books on yoga, spirituality, and the Vedas, which have become classics in the field.

Banaras has also been home to many great musicians and poets, who were also spiritual teachers. The poet-saint Kabir, who lived in the 15th century, was one of the most influential spiritual teachers in Banaras. His teachings were centered on the concept of unity and the rejection of religious dogma. His poetry has had a profound impact on the spiritual and cultural landscape of India.

The tradition of the Guru-Shishya Parampara is still alive and well in Banaras. The city is home to many spiritual teachers and their disciples, who continue to pass on the knowledge and practices of their tradition. The city is also home to many ashrams and spiritual centers, which provide a space for spiritual learning and practice.

The tradition of the Guru-Shishya Parampara is not limited to the spiritual domain but has also been instrumental in the transmission of knowledge and skills in other fields, such as music, dance, and martial arts. In Banaras, the tradition of the Guru-Shishya Parampara has played a significant role in the preservation and transmission of the city's cultural heritage.

In conclusion, the tradition of the Guru-Shishya Parampara has been a vital aspect of Indian culture and spirituality for thousands of years. Banaras has been one of the most important centers for this tradition, and it has been home to many great spiritual teachers who have left a lasting legacy on the city and the world. The tradition of the Guru-Shishya Parampara is still alive and well in Banaras, and it continues to play a significant role in the transmission of spiritual and cultural knowledge and practices.

ᢒᢒᢒ

"In Varanasi, the River Ganges flows not just with water, but with the essence of divinity."

❧❧❧

EIGHT

AYURVEDA AND YOGA IN BANARAS: ANCIENT WELLNESS TRADITIONS

Banaras is known for its rich spiritual and cultural heritage, which includes ancient wellness traditions like Ayurveda and Yoga. These traditions have been practiced in India for thousands of years and are based on the belief that wellness is achieved by maintaining a balance between the mind, body, and spirit.

Ayurveda is a holistic system of medicine that originated in India more than 5,000 years ago. It is based on the belief that health and wellness are the result of a balance between the body, mind, and spirit. According to Ayurveda, every individual is unique, and the key to good health is to understand their unique body type and make lifestyle choices that are in harmony with it.

In Banaras, Ayurveda is an integral part of daily life, and there are many Ayurvedic clinics and centers where people can receive treatments for various ailments. The city is also home to the

Institute of Medical Sciences at Banaras Hindu University, which offers a comprehensive Ayurvedic education and research program.

Yoga is another ancient wellness tradition that originated in India more than 5,000 years ago. It is a system of physical and mental exercises that aims to promote balance, flexibility, and strength in the body, as well as peace and clarity in the mind. Yoga is based on the belief that the body and mind are interconnected, and by practicing yoga, one can achieve a state of physical and mental harmony.

Banaras is known as a center for the study and practice of yoga, and there are many yoga schools and ashrams in the city. These institutions offer classes and workshops for people of all skill levels, from beginners to advanced practitioners. Many of these institutions also offer yoga teacher training programs for those who want to become certified yoga instructors.

One of the most famous yoga schools in Banaras is the Sivananda Yoga Vedanta Dhanwantari Ashram. Founded by Swami Sivananda, the ashram is dedicated to the practice and teachings of yoga, Ayurveda, and Vedanta. The ashram offers various yoga courses and teacher training programs, as well as Ayurvedic treatments and consultations.

Ayurveda and yoga are not just wellness practices in Banaras, but they are deeply ingrained in the culture and spirituality of the city. The practice of Ayurveda and yoga is believed to be a path to spiritual awakening and self-realization, and it is often integrated into other spiritual practices such as meditation and chanting.

In addition to Ayurveda and yoga, Banaras is also known for its traditional medicine practices, such as Unani and Siddha medicine. These practices have been used in India for thousands of years and are based on natural remedies and treatments.

The use of medicinal plants and herbs is also an essential part of Ayurveda and traditional medicine in Banaras. Many of these plants and herbs are grown locally and are used in Ayurvedic treatments and remedies. The city is also home to many herb gardens and medicinal plant nurseries, which are used for research and education purposes.

In conclusion, Ayurveda and yoga are ancient wellness traditions that are deeply ingrained in the culture and spirituality of Banaras. These practices are believed to be a path to spiritual awakening and self-realization, and they are an essential part of daily life in the city. Banaras is home to many Ayurvedic clinics, yoga schools, and ashrams, which offer treatments, classes, and teacher training programs. The practice of Ayurveda and yoga, along with other traditional medicine practices, is an essential part of the city's heritage and continues to play an important role in the wellness of its people.

"Banaras is a city of contrasts, a city where life and death exist side by side, where the mundane and the divine coexist in perfect harmony."

Deepak Chopra

ᏋᏋᏋ

NINE

BANARAS SILK: A TIMELESS ARTISANAL CRAFT

Banaras is famous for its rich cultural and artistic heritage, which includes its beautiful Banaras silk textiles. Banaras silk, also known as Benarasi silk, is a luxurious and high-quality silk fabric that is handwoven by skilled artisans in the city of Banaras.

The history of Banaras silk dates back to the Mughal era, when the art of silk weaving was brought to India by Persian artisans. It was during the 17th century that Banaras became a center of silk weaving, and the Banarasi silk industry began to flourish. The art of silk weaving has been passed down from generation to generation, and today, it is still an essential part of Banaras' rich cultural heritage.

The process of making Banaras silk is a labor-intensive one and involves several steps. The first step is the preparation of the silk threads, which are dyed in different colors using natural dyes. The threads are then arranged on the loom, and the weaving process begins. The weaving is done by hand, using a traditional wooden loom, and it can take several days or even weeks to complete a single piece of Banaras silk fabric.

Banaras silk is known for its intricate designs and patterns, which are woven directly into the fabric. The designs are inspired by Indian culture and mythology, and they often include images of gods and goddesses, floral motifs, and geometric patterns. The designs are often created using gold and silver threads, which add to the luxuriousness of the fabric.

There are many different types of Banaras silk fabrics, each with its own unique qualities and characteristics. The most common type is the pure silk Banarasi saree, which is known for its rich colors, intricate designs, and luxurious feel. Other types of Banaras silk fabrics include silk brocade, silk georgette, silk crepe, and silk chiffon.

Banaras silk is not only popular in India but is also renowned worldwide for its beauty and quality. It is often worn by brides and is considered a symbol of elegance and sophistication. Many fashion designers around the world have been inspired by Banaras silk and have incorporated it into their designs.

The Banaras silk industry plays an essential role in the economy of the city, providing employment to thousands of artisans and weavers. The government has recognized the importance of this industry and has taken steps to protect and promote it. In 2009, Banaras silk was granted Geographical Indication (GI) status, which recognizes it as a unique and valuable product of the region.

In recent years, there has been a growing demand for sustainable and ethical fashion, and the Banaras silk industry has responded to this trend by adopting eco-friendly practices. Many weavers now use organic silk and natural dyes, and some have even switched to solar-powered looms to reduce their carbon footprint.

In conclusion, Banaras silk is a timeless artisanal craft that is an essential part of the city's rich cultural heritage. The process of making Banaras silk is a labor-intensive one that involves skilled artisans and traditional handloom weaving techniques. The intricate designs and patterns of Banaras silk are inspired by Indian culture and mythology and are woven directly into the fabric. Banaras silk is renowned worldwide for its beauty and quality and is considered a symbol of elegance and sophistication. The Banaras silk industry provides employment to thousands of artisans and weavers and plays an essential role in the economy of the city.

"Banaras is a city that has inspired generations of
artists, writers, and musicians with its timeless
beauty and spiritual energy."

Anoushka Shankar

༄༄༄

TEN

THE MELTING POT OF RELIGIONS: COEXISTENCE AND TOLERANCE IN BANARAS

Banaras, also known as Varanasi, is a city steeped in history and spirituality, and is known as the melting pot of religions. The city has been a center of Hinduism, Buddhism, and Jainism, as well as a significant center of Islamic culture. The coexistence and tolerance of these different religious beliefs and practices have been at the heart of Banaras for centuries.

At the heart of Banaras lies the holy river Ganges, which is considered to be the lifeline of the city. The city is dotted with numerous temples, mosques, and other places of worship. The Kashi Vishwanath Temple is one of the most significant Hindu temples in the city and is dedicated to Lord Shiva. The temple is visited by thousands of devotees every day who come to seek blessings from Lord Shiva. The temple complex also houses other smaller temples dedicated to various deities.

The city is also home to several mosques, including the Gyanvapi Mosque, which was built in the 17th century by the Mughal emperor Aurangzeb. The mosque is situated near the Kashi Vishwanath Temple and is a testament to the city's rich history of interfaith harmony. It is said that the mosque was built on the site of a Hindu temple, and even today, there are remnants of the temple within the mosque complex. Despite this, both Hindus and Muslims continue to pray at the mosque and the temple, highlighting the city's culture of tolerance and coexistence.

The city also has a significant presence of Buddhism, with several Buddhist monasteries and temples located within and around the city. Sarnath, a small town located just outside of Banaras, is considered to be one of the holiest Buddhist sites in the world. It is believed that it was in Sarnath that Lord Buddha gave his first sermon, and the town is home to several important Buddhist sites, including the Dhamek Stupa and the Mulagandha Kuti Vihar.

Jainism also has a significant presence in Banaras, with several Jain temples located within the city. The most significant Jain temple in the city is the Shri Parshvanath Digambar Jain Mandir, which is dedicated to Lord Parshvanath, the 23rd Tirthankara of Jainism. The temple is visited by several Jain devotees who come to seek blessings and offer prayers.

Despite the city's significant religious diversity, there have been instances of religious tensions and conflicts in the past. However, the people of Banaras have always found a way to resolve these conflicts through dialogue and mutual understanding, thereby preserving the city's culture of tolerance and coexistence.

The city's culture of tolerance and coexistence is also reflected in its festivals and celebrations. The city celebrates several festivals throughout the year, including Diwali, Holi, Dussehra, and Eid, among others. During these festivals, people of different religious beliefs come together to celebrate and share their joy and happiness, highlighting the city's spirit of unity in diversity.

In conclusion, Banaras is a city that has been a center of various religions and spiritual traditions for centuries. The coexistence and tolerance of these different religious beliefs and practices have been at the heart of the city's culture and history. Despite the occasional religious tensions, the people of Banaras have always found a way to resolve conflicts through dialogue and mutual understanding, thereby preserving the city's culture of tolerance and coexistence. The city's rich cultural heritage and spiritual traditions continue to attract visitors from all over the world, making it a truly unique and special place.

"Banaras is a city that is as mysterious as it is enchanting, a city that is both overwhelming and liberating at the same time."

Sadhguru

ELEVEN

BANARAS: THE CENTER OF HINDU PHILOSOPHY AND LITERATURE

Banaras, also known as Varanasi, is considered to be the center of Hindu philosophy and literature. The city has been a hub of intellectual and spiritual activities for centuries, attracting scholars, philosophers, and spiritual seekers from all over the world. The city's rich cultural heritage and spiritual traditions have made it a significant center for the study and practice of Hinduism.

At the heart of Banaras lies the holy river Ganges, which is considered to be the lifeline of the city. The river is not only a source of water but also a source of spiritual purification for millions of people who come to the city every year. The riverfront of Banaras is lined with several ghats, or steps, where people gather to take a dip in the river and offer prayers to the gods and goddesses. The ghats of Banaras have been the center of several spiritual and cultural activities for centuries and have played a significant role in the city's cultural and intellectual heritage.

The city is also home to several important Hindu temples, including the Kashi Vishwanath Temple, which is dedicated to Lord Shiva. The temple is one of the most significant Hindu temples in the country and is visited by thousands of devotees every day who come to seek blessings from Lord Shiva. The temple complex also houses other smaller temples dedicated to various deities.

The city's spiritual and intellectual heritage is also reflected in its literary tradition. Banaras has been a center of Sanskrit learning for centuries, and several prominent scholars and philosophers have studied and taught here. The city is home to the Banaras Hindu University, one of the largest and most prestigious universities in India, which has played a significant role in promoting and preserving the city's cultural and intellectual heritage.

The city has been a center of Hindu philosophy and literature, with several prominent scholars and philosophers having lived and taught here. Some of the most significant works of Hindu philosophy, including the Upanishads and the Bhagavad Gita, were composed in Banaras. The city has also been home to several prominent poets and writers, including the famous Hindi poet Kabir, who lived and wrote here in the 15th century.

Banaras has also been a center of music and the performing arts, with several prominent musicians, dancers, and actors having hailed from the city. The city has a rich tradition of classical music, with several prominent musicians having performed and taught here. The Banaras Gharana, a style of Indian classical music, originated in the city and has produced several prominent musicians over the years.

In conclusion, Banaras is a city that has played a significant role in the development and preservation of Hindu philosophy and literature. The city's rich cultural and intellectual heritage has made it a significant center for the study and practice of Hinduism. The city's spiritual and cultural traditions continue to attract scholars, philosophers, and spiritual seekers from all over the world, making it a truly unique and special place. The city's literary and musical traditions have also contributed significantly to its cultural and intellectual heritage, making it a center of learning and creativity. Banaras is truly the center of Hindu philosophy and literature and continues to inspire and enlighten people from all walks of life.

*"Banaras is a city that has the power to transform,
to heal, and to awaken the soul."*

Radhanath Swami

❦❦❦

SARNATH: THE BIRTHPLACE OF BUDDHISM

Sarnath, located just a few kilometers from the ancient city of Banaras, is one of the most important Buddhist pilgrimage sites in the world. The site is known as the birthplace of Buddhism, as it was here that the Buddha gave his first sermon after attaining enlightenment.

Sarnath has a rich and ancient history, dating back to the 3rd century BCE. The site was an important center of learning and scholarship for several centuries, and several prominent Buddhist monasteries and universities were located here. The city's importance as a center of Buddhist learning and culture declined after the decline of Buddhism in India, but the site continued to be a significant pilgrimage site for Buddhists from all over the world.

The main attraction at Sarnath is the Dhamek Stupa, a massive cylindrical structure that stands at a height of 43.6 meters. The stupa was built during the Mauryan period and is believed to mark the spot where the Buddha gave his first sermon. The stupa is adorned with intricate carvings and inscriptions that depict scenes from the life of the Buddha and other important Buddhist figures.

Apart from the Dhamek Stupa, Sarnath is home to several other important Buddhist monuments and temples. The Mulagandha Kuti Vihar Temple, located just a short distance from the Dhamek Stupa, is a prominent temple that is dedicated to the Buddha. The temple is known for its beautiful frescoes and murals that depict scenes from the life of the Buddha and other important Buddhist figures.

Another prominent monument at Sarnath is the Ashoka Pillar, which is believed to have been built by the Mauryan emperor Ashoka in the 3rd century BCE. The pillar is carved with several edicts that were written by Ashoka, and is believed to have been a significant site for Buddhist pilgrimage during the Mauryan period.

Sarnath also has a rich and vibrant cultural and artistic heritage. The city is home to several important museums and galleries that showcase the city's ancient and modern art and culture. The Sarnath Museum, located near the Dhamek Stupa, is a prominent museum that houses several important artifacts and relics from the Buddhist period.

The city's cultural heritage is also reflected in its festivals and events. The city celebrates several important Buddhist festivals, including Buddha Purnima, which marks the birth, enlightenment, and death of the Buddha. The festival is celebrated with great fervor and enthusiasm, with thousands of pilgrims and tourists visiting the city to participate in the festivities.

In conclusion, Sarnath is a city of great spiritual and historical significance. The city's rich and ancient heritage as the birthplace of Buddhism has made it a significant pilgrimage site for Buddhists from all over the world. The city's monuments and temples are not only important historical and archaeological sites but also places of great spiritual significance. The city's rich cultural heritage and vibrant artistic traditions continue to attract scholars, artists, and spiritual seekers from all over the world, making it a truly unique and special place. Sarnath is a testament to the enduring legacy of Buddhism in India and continues to inspire and enlighten people from all walks of life.

ᐳᐳᐳ

*"Banaras is a city where the spirit of India resides,
a city that has been the cultural capital of the
country for centuries."*

Vikram Seth

❦❦❦

THIRTEEN

Exploring Banaras on Foot: Hidden Gems and Secret Alleys

Exploring Banaras on foot is a unique and rewarding experience. The ancient city is a labyrinth of narrow alleys, hidden courtyards, and secret lanes that are best explored on foot. Walking through the streets of Banaras is like taking a journey through time, with the city's rich history and culture evident in every nook and cranny.

One of the best ways to explore Banaras on foot is to take a guided walking tour. There are several local tour operators who offer walking tours of the city, taking visitors on a journey through the city's most historic and culturally significant sites.

One of the most popular walking tours is the Old City Heritage Walk, which takes visitors through the heart of Banaras' historic old town. The tour starts at the famous Dashashwamedh Ghat, one of the city's most important bathing ghats, and takes visitors through narrow alleys and lanes that are lined with centuries-old buildings, temples, and shrines. Along the way, visitors can explore hidden courtyards, visit small temples and shrines, and learn about the city's rich history and culture.

Another popular walking tour is the Food Walk, which takes visitors on a culinary journey through Banaras' vibrant street food scene. The tour takes visitors through the city's bustling markets and bazaars, where they can sample a wide variety of local delicacies, including chaat, lassi, and jalebi. Along the way, visitors can also learn about the city's rich culinary traditions and the importance of food in the local culture.

One of the highlights of exploring Banaras on foot is discovering the city's hidden gems and secret alleys. The city is full of hidden courtyards and secret lanes that are often overlooked by visitors. One such hidden gem is the Manikarnika Ghat, one of the city's most important cremation ghats. While many visitors come to the ghat to witness the cremation rituals, few take the time to explore the surrounding area, which is full of small temples and shrines.

Another hidden gem is the Tulsi Ghat, a small ghat that is known for its stunning views of the city's skyline. The ghat is also home to several small temples and shrines, including the famous Tulsi Manas Temple, which is dedicated to the poet Tulsidas.

Exploring Banaras on foot also offers visitors the opportunity to interact with the city's vibrant and diverse community. The city is home to people from all walks of life, including Sadhus, or holy men, who can often be seen wandering through the streets in their distinctive orange robes. Visitors can also interact with local shopkeepers and vendors, who are always happy to share stories and insights about the city's rich history and culture.

In conclusion, exploring Banaras on foot is a unique and rewarding experience that offers visitors the opportunity to discover the city's hidden gems and secret alleys. Walking through the streets of Banaras is like taking a journey through time, with the city's rich history and culture evident in every nook and cranny. Whether it's taking a heritage walk, a food tour, or simply wandering through the city's winding alleys, exploring Banaras on foot is an unforgettable experience that offers a glimpse into the heart and soul of this ancient and spiritual city.

"Banaras is a city of temples, of holy men and women, of scholars and artists, a city that embodies the essence of India."

Wendy Doniger

ᐅᐅᐅ

FOURTEEN

THE POWER OF DEVOTION: SADHUS AND NAGA BABAS OF BANARAS

The city of Banaras is home to some of the most fascinating and enigmatic people in India: the Sadhus and Naga Babas. These holy men are a living embodiment of devotion, renunciation, and spirituality, and are an integral part of the city's rich cultural heritage. In this chapter, we will explore the power of devotion that these Sadhus and Naga Babas possess and the important role they play in the spiritual fabric of Banaras.

Sadhus and Naga Babas are ascetic wanderers who have renounced worldly pleasures and material possessions in search of spiritual enlightenment. They live a life of celibacy, austerity, and discipline, and are considered to be among the most revered and respected people in Indian society. Sadhus and Naga Babas can be seen wandering the streets of Banaras, clad in orange robes, smeared with ash, and adorned with rudraksha beads.

One of the most important aspects of Sadhus and Naga Babas' lives is their devotion to the divine. They worship Lord Shiva, the Hindu god of destruction and transformation, and believe that by renouncing worldly pleasures and dedicating themselves to spiritual practice, they can attain liberation from the cycle of birth and death.

The Sadhus and Naga Babas of Banaras are known for their unique rituals and practices, which are steeped in symbolism and mysticism. One such practice is the use of cannabis, which is believed to help Sadhus and Naga Babas attain a heightened state of consciousness and connect with the divine. They also practice yoga, meditation, and other forms of spiritual discipline to deepen their devotion and connect with the divine.

The Naga Babas, in particular, are known for their fierce devotion and their association with Lord Shiva. They are often seen carrying tridents, wearing tiger skins, and sporting dreadlocks, which are believed to symbolize their connection to the divine. The Naga Babas also participate in the Kumbh Mela, the largest religious gathering in the world, where they perform ritualistic practices and take a dip in the holy waters of the Ganges.

The Sadhus and Naga Babas of Banaras also play an important role in the spiritual and social life of the city. They are often consulted for their wisdom and guidance, and are considered to be spiritual advisors to the people of Banaras. They are also involved in philanthropic activities and work to improve the lives of the poor and disadvantaged.

However, the life of a Sadhu or Naga Baba is not without its challenges. They face criticism from some quarters of society, who view their renunciation of material possessions as a form of escapism. They are also vulnerable to exploitation, as many people seek their blessings and guidance in exchange for money and gifts.

Despite these challenges, the Sadhus and Naga Babas of Banaras continue to be an important part of the city's cultural and spiritual heritage. Their devotion, discipline, and dedication to the divine inspire awe and reverence among the people of Banaras and beyond. They are a reminder that the power of devotion can transform lives, and that true spirituality is not about material possessions or external rituals, but about inner transformation and connection with the divine.

ৡৡৡ

"Banaras is a city that has been a beacon of spirituality, knowledge, and culture for thousands of years, a city that has withstood the test of time."

Sri Sri Ravi Shankar

FIFTEEN

BANARAS AT NIGHT: A MYSTICAL EXPERIENCE

Banaras, also known as Varanasi, is a city that is steeped in history, tradition, and spirituality. It is a city that is alive with energy and activity, and nowhere is this more evident than at night. As the sun sets and darkness falls, Banaras undergoes a transformation, becoming a place of mystery, magic, and mysticism. In this chapter, we will explore Banaras at night, and the mystical experience that it offers.

The night-time atmosphere of Banaras is like no other. The sound of temple bells, the chanting of mantras, and the aroma of incense fill the air. The narrow, winding lanes of the old city are lit up by the warm glow of oil lamps, and the waters of the Ganges are illuminated by the flickering flames of diyas (small earthen lamps).

One of the most captivating experiences of Banaras at night is the evening aarti ceremony, held on the banks of the Ganges. The aarti is a ritual offering of light, fire, and water, and is a beautiful and moving experience. It is conducted by priests, who wave oil lamps and incense sticks, while chanting mantras in praise of the gods and goddesses. The aarti is a time when the people of Banaras come together to offer their prayers and gratitude to the divine, and the atmosphere is one of reverence and devotion.

Another mystical experience of Banaras at night is the boat ride on the Ganges. As you glide along the river, the reflections of the flickering diyas create a shimmering, magical effect on the water. The boat ride is a time for reflection and contemplation, as you take in the sights and sounds of the city from a unique perspective. The boat ride also offers a glimpse into the lives of the people who live along the river, as you pass by the ghats (riverfront steps) where they go to perform their daily rituals.

The ghats of Banaras are also a fascinating place to explore at night. The ghats are a series of steps leading down to the Ganges, and are used by the people of Banaras for bathing, washing clothes, and performing religious ceremonies. At night, the ghats take on a new life, as the sounds of drums and cymbals fill the air, and the people gather to offer their prayers and devotions. It is a time when the barriers between the physical and spiritual worlds seem to dissolve, and the mystical nature of Banaras is at its most potent.

One of the most famous ghats of Banaras is the Manikarnika Ghat, which is also known as the "Burning Ghat." It is the place where the bodies of the deceased are brought to be cremated, in accordance with Hindu tradition. At night, the Manikarnika Ghat takes on a surreal quality, as the flames from the cremations illuminate the night sky, and the chanting of mantras fills the air. It is a place that is both somber and awe-inspiring, and is a reminder of the cyclical nature of life and death.

In conclusion, Banaras at night is a mystical experience that is not to be missed. It is a time when the city comes alive with energy and activity, and the barriers between the physical and spiritual worlds seem to dissolve. The evening aarti, the boat ride on the Ganges, and the ghats of Banaras all offer a glimpse into the spiritual heart of the city, and the power of devotion and faith. Banaras at night is a truly unforgettable experience that will leave a lasting impression on anyone who experiences it.

Varanasi is a city that will test your limits, but also teach you to transcend them."

❥❥❥

SIXTEEN

THE INTERSECTION OF SCIENCE AND SPIRITUALITY IN BANARAS

Banaras, also known as Varanasi, is a city that is renowned for its spirituality and rich cultural heritage. However, it is also a city that has played a significant role in the history of science and technology. The intersection of science and spirituality in Banaras has been a topic of discussion for many years, and in this chapter, we will explore the relationship between the two and how they coexist in Banaras.

One of the most famous examples of the intersection of science and spirituality in Banaras is the ancient system of Ayurveda. Ayurveda is an ancient Indian system of medicine that has been practiced for thousands of years. It is a holistic system that treats the body, mind, and spirit, and emphasizes the importance of balance and harmony in all aspects of life. Banaras is home to many Ayurvedic clinics and hospitals, where visitors can receive treatment from trained practitioners.

Another example of the intersection of science and spirituality in Banaras is the study of yoga and meditation. Yoga and meditation have been practiced in India for thousands of years, and have gained popularity all over the world in recent years. Yoga and meditation have been proven to have numerous physical and mental health benefits, and many studies have been conducted on their efficacy. Banaras is home to many yoga and meditation centers, where visitors can learn and practice these ancient techniques.

The study of astronomy and astrology is also deeply intertwined with the spiritual traditions of Banaras. In ancient times, the city was renowned for its astronomical knowledge, and many important astronomical observations were made here. The Jantar Mantar, an observatory built in the 18th century, is a testament to the city's scientific heritage. In addition, astrology has been an important part of Indian culture for thousands of years, and many people in Banaras consult astrologers for guidance on important life decisions.

The study of religion and philosophy is another area where science and spirituality intersect in Banaras. The city is home to many religious and philosophical traditions, including Hinduism, Buddhism, Jainism, and Sikhism. Many scholars and researchers have studied these traditions in depth, examining their historical and cultural significance, as well as their philosophical and scientific underpinnings.

The Banaras Hindu University is another important institution that reflects the intersection of science and spirituality in Banaras. Founded in 1916, the university is one of the largest residential universities in Asia, and is known for its academic excellence in a wide range of fields, including science, technology, medicine, and the arts. The university also has a strong emphasis on spirituality and the study of religion and philosophy, and offers courses in yoga, meditation, and Ayurveda.

In conclusion, the intersection of science and spirituality in Banaras is a testament to the city's rich cultural heritage and intellectual tradition. The study of ancient systems of medicine, yoga and meditation, astronomy and astrology, and religion and philosophy are all areas where science and spirituality intersect in Banaras. The city's history and culture provide a unique backdrop for the study of these areas, and the city's institutions, including the Banaras Hindu University, provide opportunities for students and scholars to explore these topics in depth. The intersection of science and spirituality in Banaras is a dynamic and ever-evolving area of study, and will continue to be a source of fascination and inquiry for years to come.

"Banaras is a city where the past is present, where the ancient and the modern blend seamlessly."

Aishwarya Rai Bachchan

SEVENTEEN

FOOD AND FESTIVALS OF BANARAS: A CULTURAL DELIGHT

Food and festivals are an integral part of the cultural heritage of Banaras. The city is renowned for its delectable food and vibrant festivals, which reflect the diversity and richness of its cultural traditions. In this chapter, we will explore the unique and delicious cuisine of Banaras and the colorful festivals that are celebrated throughout the year.

Cuisine of Banaras:

Banaras is a food lover's paradise, with a diverse range of dishes that cater to every palate. The city's cuisine is a reflection of its rich cultural heritage, and draws influences from the Mughal, British, and Hindu traditions. The food in Banaras is known for its distinct flavors, spices, and textures, which are the result of a careful blend of traditional cooking techniques and local ingredients.

One of the most famous dishes in Banaras is the chaat, which is a savory snack made from a mix of boiled potatoes, chickpeas, spices, and tamarind chutney. The dish is typically served with crispy fried puris and yogurt, and is a favorite of locals and tourists alike. Other popular dishes in Banaras include samosas, kachoris, lassi, and thandai, which are all made from local ingredients and prepared using traditional cooking methods.

The cuisine of Banaras is also heavily influenced by the religious and spiritual traditions of the city. Many of the dishes served in Banaras are vegetarian, as a result of the Hindu belief in ahimsa, or non-violence. The city is also known for its unique food rituals, such as the daily feeding of cows and monkeys, which is considered to be a form of charity and good karma.

Festivals of Banaras:

Banaras is a city that celebrates its festivals with great fervor and enthusiasm. The city is home to many festivals throughout the year, each of which has its own unique traditions and customs. Some of the most famous festivals in Banaras include:

Dev Diwali: Dev Diwali, also known as the festival of lights, is celebrated in the month of November. The festival marks the victory of Lord Shiva over the demon Tripurasura and is celebrated by lighting thousands of diyas on the banks of the Ganges River.

Maha Shivratri: Maha Shivratri is celebrated in the month of February and is dedicated to Lord Shiva. The festival is celebrated with great devotion and includes offerings of bael leaves, milk, and fruits to Lord Shiva.

Durga Puja: Durga Puja is a five-day festival that is celebrated in the month of October. The festival celebrates the victory of Goddess Durga over the demon Mahishasura and is marked by the installation of beautiful pandals and idols throughout the city.

Holi: Holi is a festival of colors that is celebrated in the month of March. The festival is marked by the throwing of colors and water on friends and family, and is a celebration of love and unity.

In addition to these festivals, Banaras is also known for its music and dance traditions, which are an integral part of many of the city's celebrations.

In conclusion, the food and festivals of Banaras are a true cultural delight. The city's cuisine is a reflection of its diverse cultural traditions and draws influences from the Mughal, British, and Hindu traditions. The festivals in Banaras are celebrated with great enthusiasm and provide a unique opportunity to experience the rich cultural heritage of the city. Whether it's the delectable chaat or the vibrant celebrations of Dev Diwali, Banaras is a city that is sure to tantalize your taste buds and capture your heart.

▷▷▷

"Banaras is a city where every corner is infused
with the divine, where every moment is a spiritual
experience."

Jaggi Vasudev

❦❦❦

EIGHTEEN

THE ARTISTIC TREASURES OF BANARAS: PAINTINGS, SCULPTURES, AND HANDICRAFTS

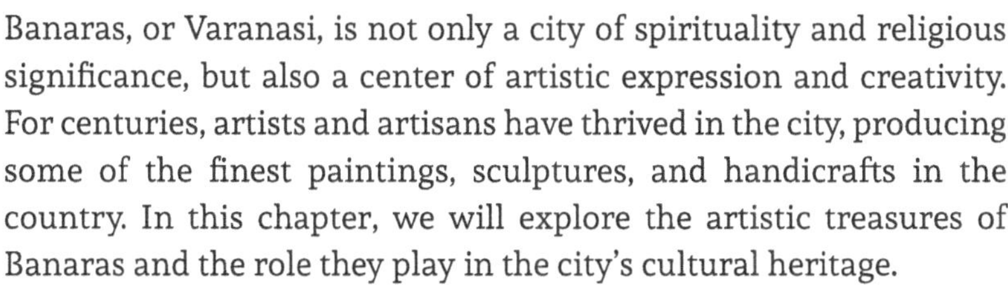

Banaras, or Varanasi, is not only a city of spirituality and religious significance, but also a center of artistic expression and creativity. For centuries, artists and artisans have thrived in the city, producing some of the finest paintings, sculptures, and handicrafts in the country. In this chapter, we will explore the artistic treasures of Banaras and the role they play in the city's cultural heritage.

Paintings

Banaras has a long tradition of producing exquisite paintings, many of which depict religious and mythological themes. The most famous style of painting from the region is the Mughal-inspired Banaras School, which emerged in the 17th century under the patronage of the local Mughal governors. The style is characterized by its use of bold colors, intricate detailing, and an emphasis on portraiture. The paintings often depict scenes from the Ramayana and Mahabharata epics, as well as portraits of rulers, nobles, and other important figures.

Another style of painting that emerged in Banaras is the Kachni style, which features vibrant colors and intricate designs. This style is often used to decorate walls and floors of homes, as well as for making decorative items such as boxes, trays, and other household items.

Sculptures

Banaras is home to some of the most beautiful and intricate sculptures in India. The city has been a center of sculpting since ancient times, and the tradition continues to this day. The most famous type of sculpture produced in Banaras is the Shiva Lingam, a sacred symbol of Lord Shiva. The city is also known for its stone carvings, which adorn temples and other public buildings.

One of the most famous sculptors of Banaras was the legendary artist Ram Chandra, who lived in the 18th century. He was known for his intricate carvings of Hindu deities, which are still revered today.

Handicrafts

Banaras is also known for its handicrafts, which include textiles, metalwork, and woodwork. The city has a long tradition of weaving, and Banarasi silk is one of the most famous textiles in the world. The silk is made using a special technique that involves weaving gold and silver threads into the fabric, resulting in a shimmering effect.

Metalwork is another important handicraft in Banaras, and the city is known for its brassware and copperware. The metalwork often features intricate designs and engravings, and is used to make items such as lamps, utensils, and decorative pieces.

Woodwork is another important handicraft in Banaras, and the city is known for its intricately carved wooden furniture and decorative items. The woodwork often features religious and mythological themes, as well as intricate floral and geometric designs.

Conclusion

Banaras is a city of immense artistic richness and cultural heritage. Its artistic treasures are a testament to the creativity and skill of its artists and artisans, and are an integral part of the city's identity. The paintings, sculptures, and handicrafts produced in Banaras are not only beautiful, but also serve as important cultural artifacts that connect the present with the past. Visitors to Banaras should take the time to explore the city's artistic treasures and appreciate the skill and artistry of its craftsmen.

ᐖᐖᐖ

"Banaras is a city of contrasts, of contradictions, and of complexities, a city that is both chaotic and serene."

Arundhati Roy

NINETEEN

BANARAS BEYOND BORDERS: THE GLOBAL REACH OF SPIRITUALITY

Banaras, also known as Varanasi, is a city that holds a special place in the hearts of many people around the world. It is one of the oldest continuously inhabited cities in the world and has been a center of spiritual and cultural activities for centuries. People from all corners of the world come to Banaras to experience its mystical atmosphere and to connect with their spirituality. Banaras has a unique charm that transcends borders, and its spirituality has a global reach.

The city has always been a destination for spiritual seekers, scholars, and artists from around the world. The ancient university of Banaras, also known as the Benares Hindu University, has been a hub of academic activities for more than a century. The university attracts students and scholars from all over India and abroad, who come to study various aspects of Indian philosophy, religion, art, and culture. The university has produced many great scholars, scientists, and artists who have made a significant contribution to their respective fields.

Banaras has always been a melting pot of cultures, religions, and traditions. Over the centuries, people from different parts of the world have come to Banaras, bringing with them their own beliefs, customs, and practices. The city has absorbed these diverse influences, creating a unique blend of spirituality that is open and inclusive. Banaras has a long history of tolerance and acceptance, and this spirit of openness has helped to create a vibrant and diverse community that welcomes people from all over the world.

The spiritual and cultural richness of Banaras has attracted many people from the West who are seeking spiritual enlightenment. The city has become a hub for yoga, meditation, and other spiritual practices that have gained popularity around the world. Many yoga schools, meditation centers, and spiritual retreats have sprung up in Banaras, offering a range of programs and services to people from different parts of the world. These institutions provide a platform for people to explore their spirituality and to connect with like-minded individuals from different cultures and backgrounds.

Banaras has also been a source of inspiration for many Western artists and writers who have been drawn to its mystical atmosphere and ancient traditions. The city has been depicted in countless works of literature, art, and music, and its influence can be seen in the works of many great artists and writers. The spiritual and cultural heritage of Banaras has also inspired many Westerners to explore Indian spirituality, philosophy, and culture, leading to a deeper understanding and appreciation of the diversity and richness of Indian traditions.

Banaras has become a center of attraction for tourists from around the world. The city's rich cultural heritage, ancient temples, and spiritual atmosphere have made it a popular destination for travelers seeking an authentic spiritual experience. The city's ancient history, traditions, and spirituality continue to fascinate people from all over the world, drawing them to Banaras in search of spiritual enlightenment and cultural immersion.

In recent years, the city has become more accessible to visitors from around the world, with better transportation links, improved infrastructure, and a growing range of accommodation options. This has helped to boost tourism in the city and has made it easier for people from different parts of the world to experience the spiritual and cultural richness of Banaras.

In conclusion, Banaras has a global reach that extends far beyond its physical borders. Its spiritual and cultural richness has attracted people from all corners of the world, creating a diverse and vibrant community that celebrates the diversity of human experience. The city's spirit of openness and acceptance has helped to create a unique blend of spirituality that transcends borders and speaks to the universal human experience. Banaras is truly a city of the world, a place where people from different cultures, religions, and traditions can come together to connect with their spirituality and to celebrate the richness of human experience.

"Banaras is a city that has the power to awaken the soul, to make one realize the true purpose of life."

Sadhguru

ᗡᗡᗡ

TWENTY

REFLECTIONS ON BANARAS: A PERSONAL JOURNEY OF DISCOVERY AND TRANSFORMATION

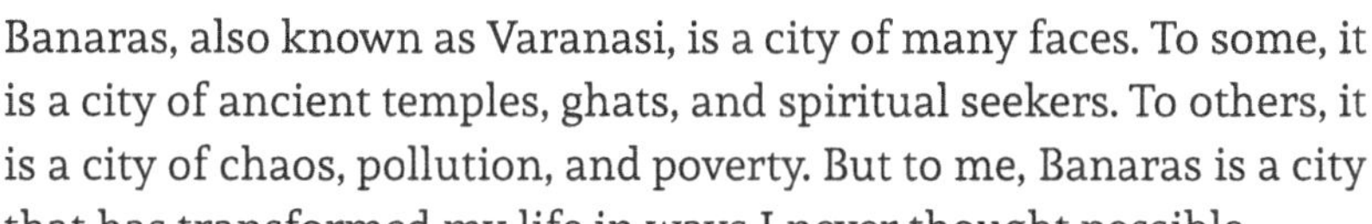

Banaras, also known as Varanasi, is a city of many faces. To some, it is a city of ancient temples, ghats, and spiritual seekers. To others, it is a city of chaos, pollution, and poverty. But to me, Banaras is a city that has transformed my life in ways I never thought possible.

I first visited Banaras as a tourist, curious to explore its rich history and culture. I wandered through the narrow alleys, marveling at the intricate carvings on the temples and the bustling crowds of people. I witnessed the famous Ganga Aarti ceremony, where priests offer prayers to the river Ganges, and watched as thousands of devotees took a dip in the sacred waters.

But it wasn't until I started interacting with the locals that I began to see Banaras in a new light. I met Sadhus and Naga Babas, holy men who had renounced the material world in search of spiritual liberation. They shared their stories with me, and I was struck by their unwavering faith and dedication to their beliefs.

I also met ordinary people who had been living in Banaras for generations. They invited me into their homes, shared their food with me, and told me stories about their families and their city. Through these conversations, I learned that Banaras is not just a place of spirituality, but also a place of resilience and community.

As I spent more time in Banaras, I began to realize that the city was changing me. I was becoming more patient, more accepting, and more compassionate. I started to see the world through a different lens, one that was more focused on the inner journey rather than the outer trappings of success.

I also began to understand the power of rituals and traditions. In Banaras, every ritual has a purpose, every tradition has a story. Whether it is the daily puja performed by families at their homes, or the grand processions during festivals, every act is imbued with meaning and significance. I learned that these rituals and traditions provide a sense of continuity and connection to the past, and help us to understand our place in the world.

Banaras also taught me the importance of introspection and self-reflection. The city is a place of intense self-discovery, where one is forced to confront their deepest fears and desires. Whether it is through meditation, yoga, or simply being in the presence of holy men and women, Banaras offers a space for contemplation and introspection.

As I look back on my time in Banaras, I realize that the city has left an indelible mark on me. It has taught me the power of faith, the importance of community, and the value of introspection. It has shown me that there is more to life than the pursuit of material success, and that true fulfillment comes from within.

In conclusion, Banaras is not just a city, it is a way of life. It is a city that has the power to transform and inspire, and I am grateful for the time I spent there. I hope that others will also have the opportunity to experience the magic of Banaras, and that they too will be transformed by its eternal flame of spirituality and divine connections.

ᐧᐧᐧ

"Banaras is a city that is beyond description, a city
that has to be experienced to be understood."

Ravi Shankar Prasad

ᐅᐅᐅ

References And Citations

This book has been created by referencing various websites on the internet, including Wikipedia, in order to gather valuable information and data. In addition to online sources, this book also draws upon the author's own research and includes references to relevant books in the library. By combining a variety of sources, this book provides a comprehensive and well-researched account of the subject matter. The author has taken care to ensure that all information presented is accurate and properly cited to give credit to the original sources.

Although every effort has been made to ensure the accuracy and completeness of the information presented in this book, human errors may still occur. If any reader discovers an error or omission in this book, I respectfully welcome their feedback and encourage them to bring it to my attention. Such feedback is valuable to me, and I will take all necessary steps to correct any errors and improve the content of this book in future editions. Thank you for your understanding and support.

ÞÞÞ

Contact

Aditya Gupta
C/26/10B 1 A
Senpura
Varanasi - 221 001
8756600980
aditya10sun@gmail.com

ᐅᐅᐅ

|| LOKAHA SAMASTHAHA SUKHINO BHAVANTU ||

❦❦❦